Eileen Kerr is happily married with a family of two boys, who have special needs. Having worked as a hairdresser in Ireland, New York and London, since the age of seventeen, she now owns her own hair and beauty salon at home in Northern Ireland.

She had an unhappy childhood due to her father being abusive and an alcoholic. She continued to be attracted to toxic men and had numerous undesirable relationships. She also was in a previous marriage, which she found to be abusive and controlling.

Nowadays she enjoys nothing more than walking, swimming and spending time with family and friends.

I would like to dedicate this book to my late mother Eileen, who loved me dearly through my life, my husband Stan, who loves me, supports me and encourages me, and my two sons Ben and Zec, both of who provide unconditional love and have taught me patience. I would also like to thank all of my female friends and acquaintances who over the years have helped me be aware of the characters that are the basis of my book.

Eileen Kerr

THE FOOL NO LONGER

AUSTIN MACAULEY PUBLISHERS™

LONDON • CAMBRIDGE • NEW YORK • SHARJAH

A CIP catalogue record for this title is available from the
British Library.

ISBN 9781787100893 (Paperback)
ISBN 9781787100909 (E-Book)
www.austinmacauley.com

First Published (2017)
Austin Macauley Publishers Ltd.
25 Canada Square
Canary Wharf
London
E14 5LQ

Chapter 1
My Wakeup Call

Picture this!

It's the day before your wedding and you are asking other people, "Do you think I should get married to this person?"

Or, on your wedding day you want to keep away from your new husband as much as possible because you have realised you have made a huge mistake.

Or, your new husband tells you as you're walking down the aisle, "You will do as I say now".

Alarm bells!

How many times have us ladies been in relationships, and one or two months into the relationship, we think to ourselves 'what have I got myself into?' We know consciously that this isn't going to work out, but we hang on in there. But for what reason? Are we afraid of being on our own, or are we concerned with what other people think and how this looks like to the outside world?

Do we think Mr Perfect doesn't exist and convince ourselves that we will make do with first thing that comes along?

I remember lying in bed one night, a couple of months after my first marriage ended, at the ripe old age of thirty-four (that's how I felt at that time), thinking to myself I have one failed marriage and countless failed relationships behind me. I began to think 'the man I'm looking for just doesn't exist on this green earth.' I laughed to myself and thought right, if I had my choice of the perfect man, what would his qualities be?

Firstly, I thought, well, integrity is a very important foundation in any relationship. Next, I thought that he has to love me as much as I love him. Now that's a big ask. He must have the same moral values and lastly he has to make me laugh, goodness knows, you need a sense of humour in any relationship, especially when the chips are down. Then I thought to myself, well you can't kill the dream and nodded off to sleep.

Roll on six months later, and I was introduced to a fine species of a man, through a mutual friend of ours. Initial thoughts were, very attractive, friendly, and I discovered we had the same sense of humour.

Long story short and ten years of marriage later, I can safely say my husband is a very close Mr Perfect. There are days I could eat him, I love him that much, and other days I wish I had eaten him. Naturally enough!

Previous to meeting my husband, I met a guy who was living under the same roof as his 'ex' wife.

According to him, they were living separate lives and the only reason he stayed is because he wouldn't have as much time with his kids. Fair point, I thought, but is this the type of relationship I want? I could see this guy was never going to be able to give me 100% of his time. Rightly so, I wouldn't want somebody who had to decide between me and his kids.

I had two options. Accept things the way they are, or break up and find someone who was going to give me the time and relationship I deserved and wanted. I decided I didn't want to be 'second best' in someone's life. Thus leaving way for Mr Perfect to enter into my life.

Life isn't all roses in the garden, and no relationship is perfect. Both partners have to give 100%.

I remember years ago being told by a friend, 'Always marry for love because you need the love to get through the tough times'.

A girl I use to work with married her husband because she didn't find anybody that loved her as much or treated her as well. Even though she saw him more as a friend than a lover. They went on to have kids. While they seem very happy, I often wonder did she grow to love him or is she still with him because he is the 'safest bet'?

Another girl's boyfriend broke up with her and she married on the rebound. She had two kids and ending up drinking every day to mask the unhappiness she felt because she couldn't be with the one she truly loved.

A woman's instinct is a powerful tool.

I know quite a few women who have married for all the wrong reasons. I would say it's better to be single and happy, than to be married and miserable.

A friend of mine once had to break off an engagement because her fiancé had cheated on her. She was so tempted to go back into the relationship again. She kept telling me how much she loved him. When I told her it wasn't love, she couldn't understand what I meant. I told her my idea of love is reciprocated. It's not love if he is playing around. I often wondered if it was the bad boy in him she was attracted to in the first place.

Us women love a bad boy, a challenge. Someone we think we can eventually tame.

One night soon after I met my husband, we went out to a bar. An old male friend came over to me and threw his arms round me and said, "How's the Ice Queen tonight?" He always called me that because I wouldn't go out with him.

I could see my future husband watching the whole thing. I thought to myself, I'm going to hear about it now when this guy has finished wrapping himself around me. When he eventually dragged himself away, I turned to my right to see MFH smiling back. I said, "Are you okay?"

He replied, "Oh yes," looking like the cat that had the cream.

"Are you sure?" I said.

He said, "Oh yes, you're with me".

Well such a relief came over me. I thought, well that's a great start. He's not the jealous type. 'Tick that box'.

As I've got older, I've become stronger and I don't take as much 'drama' from men. I think that's because I'm more secure in myself. It doesn't matter to me as much now what other people think.

My late mother always said, "If in doubt, do without."

In the following chapters, my aim is to give some insight into my experiences in relationships as well as experiences of others. I have defined the chapters as types of men I have met;

Mr Controlling

Mr Narcissistic

Mr Womaniser

Mr Addictive Personality

Mr Couch Potato

Mr Miser

Mr Mummy's Boy

Mr Passive Aggressive

Mr Asperger

Mr Pinocchio

Mr Booty Call

Mr Married Man

Mr Online Dating

Mr Micro-cheat

Mr I'm Always Right

My Final Word

Love is patient. Love is kind…

A quote from *1 Corinthians 13:4*

Chapter 2
Mr Controlling

There are many types of Controlled Behaviour or Abuse.

Verbal, psychological, emotional, sexual, financial and Coercive.

If all relationships stayed the way that they were in the beginning, very few would eventually break up. Of course in the beginning when you meet someone, they just feel like 'loves young dream' and you can't believe your luck. You may meet them once during the week and part of the weekend.

That doesn't give you the full picture, unless you are 'Mystic Meg'. You aren't seeing that person on his 'bad days'. To get the full picture, I think you need to see them every day. In a lot of cases when we marry, and we have never lived with our partner beforehand, we have no idea what that person is truly about.

I don't think you fully know someone until you live with them.

It usually takes a year to get adjusted to married life. Getting to know your partner doesn't always turn out the way you thought they were. It can hit you like a ton of bricks.

In my experience, the abuser takes the following pattern:

- Depression and a dark mood that descends out of the blue.
- Physical and mental abuse hits its peak.
- Lastly, a period of calm and reconciliation commences giving false hope.

A girl once told me that her husband used to phone her at work every day, sometimes twice. He would ask her was she talking to any of her male colleagues. When she would say no, he wouldn't believe her. When she would get home, he would get volatile, slap and hit her.

In the beginning, she blamed herself, that she had caused the situation to get out of hand. Eventually he made her leave her job.

She felt that all the phone calls he made in the beginning were out of love for her. It wasn't until she left her marriage and met someone else years later, she realised that her marriage was about control and not love for her.

A hypnotherapist once told me that if someone tries to control a relationship, they don't care about it.

When my friend looks back on her relationship, she told me all the signs were there before she got married. He slapped her once when she didn't agree with him on something so trivial. Then he cried for two hours, was so sorry for what he had done, and she believed him. This is so common. When a person is crying their heart out, you feel sorry for them and are taken in by the deceit. Maybe they are sorry, but I have never known a situation like this where they slapped only once. It always happens again and escalates into more serious abuse and even death.

I remember two women who were both married to wealthy men. Each thought the other had 'the perfect life'. Driving a sports car, huge mansion and holidays several times a year. It wasn't until years later when they were both divorced and they got talking one day, that they realised that the both of them were living the same life. Married to a controlling partner.

One of the similarities they had was that their husbands demanded receipts for their grocery shopping. They had a budget and they knew they couldn't go over it. These were two wealthy men. Obviously, these women were controlled in other ways as well.

I know women whose partners went to their hairdressers and told them they had to chop their partner's hair completely short. When one hairdresser heard this, she told him she can't do that unless she gets permission from the person themselves. His reply was, "Oh, she will be getting it cut." I think this is so their partners won't be attracting any unwanted attention from the opposite sex. Partners that go to hairdressers with their partners can be another sign of control.

When I met Mr Controlling, someone said to me, "He's very good to his mother so you're unto a winner with him." It couldn't have been further from the truth. He made an excellent son but an abusive partner.

In my experience, I felt that the control over me was real love at that time. I naively thought that no one had 'our type of relationship' where he loves me so much that he takes over my life.

It can escalate gradually, that you hardly notice what is happening. He told me that he didn't like my friends, that they weren't genuine. Then it moved on to my family. Until one by one my nearest and dearest had disappeared and there was just me and him and his family and his friends. My spirit died and I felt stripped away and all life was sucked out of me.

Some nights were spent him arguing, and I knew he was keeping me awake all night as punishment for maybe not dusting the door frame or looking in the direction of another man.

I became afraid to speak for fear of getting hit. I could tell by his eyes what mood he was going to be in. They would turn black as night and I could feel my stomach churning, and I knew what was ahead of me. Even though I never left the house, I was 'having numerous affairs'. One day I was so angry, I told him that I must be 'Houdini' to be able to get out of this house. It was like Shawshank prison.

He was totally 'off the wall'. I can laugh about it now. Some of the accusations were ridiculous, anything to get a fight going. I used to tell him, "You would fight with your own shadow if I wasn't here."

I thought I was on to a winner, when I first met him, because he never drank alcohol. It was like living with a dry drunk, which was just as bad.

I knew a girl who finished with her boyfriend because he turned up on her 'girls' night out,' because he had heard she was out without him. He won her back by buying her a huge engagement ring. When she married him, things went from bad to worse. Roll on ten years later they ended up divorcing.

When a person decides to end a controlling relationship, it doesn't just end there. You could have months or years of stalking to contend with. It's like a bad smell you can't get rid of. Everywhere you go, they seem to suspiciously 'turn up.'

I was told once, "If I can't have you, then no one will". These haunting words conjure up fear of what a person could be capable of. This is a common tactic when the victim threatens to leave. This can be a life-and-death situation.

I know a couple that have been married for forty years and every now and again her husband would produce his gun discreetly, just to remind her what he told her all those years ago. To keep her 'in her place'. When they were first married he produced two bullets and told her if she ever leaves he will find her and one bullet will be for her and the other one will be for him.

Working with the public and doing their hair, I learn a lot from what they reveal and confide to me. One girl in her early twenties told me that her boyfriend punched her and she was taking him to court. Thank goodness she had the courage never to take him back. She told me some girls of her generation are willing to put up with verbal and physical abuse.

It's a hidden epidemic.

I know some women decide to stay 'for the kids'. Fear and pride can take over and they say they will leave when the kids grow up and leave home. Then, when this happens, then they think they are too old and it's too much hassle.

It so difficult to confide in friends and family, because we don't want to seem weak as we have chosen to settle for this type of life.

The 'Honeymoon Period' is a fascinating time. All be it 'short lived'. In an abusive relationship, this period is after all the turmoil and arguments etc. It's a period of time when both partners are getting on. It feels like your honeymoon all over again. He will have extreme highs and lows. When he's on a high, then you are too, because you think this time, things are different. He's going to change. But I have never known this to happen.

It's a vicious cycle and pattern, that never changes over the years. Eighty percent of the time your relationship can be good, but the other twenty can be like hell on earth.

Women who have been married for decades still feel they are to blame for everything that is wrong in their marriage. It's like a form of brain washing. If you're told something often enough, you start to believe it.

There's a saying that you teach people how to treat you. In other words, if somebody mistreats you and you stay and put up with it, then you are sending out a message, it's ok to treat me this way.

In some cases, women are pregnant before abuse begins. This could be because of jealousy over the baby.

Some women who have had controlling fathers see this as normal behaviour. Therefore, they can enter relationships that are controlling also.

I have heard of women having their car and phone bugged but only find out when they leave the relationship. Some women have said they knew when their partner had gone to their handbag the previous night, because in the morning their bag was left disturbed.

Controllers can be known to the outside world as 'Gentlemen'.

One day I had reached my, 'I've had enough' point. I asked myself, "Are you happy to live like this for the next however long we both shall live, and eventually maybe children into the equation?" I knew the answer was NO. I had visions of him killing me or vice versa. I knew I had hit rock bottom. My second time leaving was my final and I never looked back.

Four months after I left, I felt I had got my power back and I went to see him. I said a prayer before I went to ask God to protect me because I was going alone.

I told him I forgave him for all he said and done to me. His jaw dropped, he couldn't speak. He knew all ties of control were severed forever. I wished him 'all the best' and I left. I don't recommend anybody do this at all, as everybody's situation is different, and you certainly don't do this alone.

Whenever I had moments of wanting to re-enter the relationship, I would picture myself walking across the threshold again and into that 'cell of fear'. It was the one thing that got me through that period of thinking about all the 'good times'. When you are away from the abuser, your mind can easily forget the horrendous abuse you put up with, and your heart can renege on everything you felt when you walked out.

When I look back, I remember how he never told me he loved me.

It reminded me when Prince Charles was asked, was he in love with Lady Diana when they got engaged. His answer was quite telling. "Whatever love means".

You should be entering a relationship to be better off, not worse off. I mean emotionally, and in every way possible.

The three things I lived with were:

- Hope – the hope that things would change.
- Shame – too ashamed to tell family and friends.
- Fear – What am I going to do? And where am I going to go?

I have come to realise *"where there is love there is no fear"*

(a quote from *1 John 4:18*).

Chapter 3
Mr Narcissistic

When I first met Mr Narcissistic, I thought I had met my soulmate. He was everything I wanted in a partner. He promised me the sun, moon and the stars. He said all the right things and told me what I wanted to hear.

I met him in a bar one night while we were with mutual friends. We were all talking and having a laugh, when slowly he took my hand. I felt goose bumps from my head to my toes. We had an instant connection. He asked to see me again. I totally fell for him.

Narcissism can come in the form of flattery, charisma and buying you things e.g. gifts, dinners, getaways etc.

A couple of weeks into the relationship, we were out at a pub (once again) and a woman came over and started shouting. Her head was spinning like something possessed, and screaming how he had used her daughter and two-timed her. I felt so uncomfortable I hung my head thinking was I the one he two-timed her with? Suddenly I felt the need to pee (a quick get a way).

When I asked him what it was all about, he said, "Oh it's nothing (hate those words). She's just an over protective mother that can't except our relationship is over."

"I thought you had murdered her daughter the way she was getting on."

I thought to myself, I don't need this drama in my life. I've had enough drama to do me a lifetime.

He phoned me one night (two weeks into our relationship) saying that he had phoned a taxi for me so I could go and meet his family, and they were having a bar-b-q. I was taken aback! This never happened me before. It was all very uncomfortable, but he was so charming and I really liked him, so after ten minutes of persuading me, I went along with it. We saw each other every day after that.

After a few months, he seemed to change and started putting me down in front of my friends. As if he was laughing at me, rather than with me. I would feel my stomach anxious and in knots. He was making me feel uncomfortable.

Then I had a wedding to go to and we were invited, but he insisted that I should go on my own which I thought very strange. Even when I said I really wanted him to go, he said, "You will have a great time without me with all your friends."

I went ahead on my own. But something just wasn't right. Woman's instinct!

The next day my friend told me he was seen with someone and that he has a 'reputation'. Once again my stomach went into knots. When I saw him later that day, I told him he was seen with a 'blonde'. He said, "That was my friend".

I laughed. "Oh you were kissing your friend."

He knew I wasn't believing any of it.

I was all dressed up and he asked, "Where are you going?"

I said, "Well, you know that fella that gave me his number the other night you were out on lad's night out? Well I phoned him and he's picking me up in half an hour, so there's no point in hanging around ('touché')." I pointed to the door. He turned and walked out. I had made the whole thing up.

It was the hardest thing ever, gathering myself to dress up and look like I was heading out. As I watched him drive away, I burst into tears and proceeded to take my makeup off. I was devastated. I was so tempted to believe him and it would have been so easy to forget about it all.

I could just see a pattern emerging where he was spending more time with his friends and no matter what I said, he would try and put me down in a sneering way. It wasn't turning out the way I thought it was going to.

Especially when it came to sex. It didn't matter if I was feeling under the weather or had a bereavement. It was his 'right' to have it, no matter about my feelings.

He kept texting saying that he was under a lot of stress at work and he had never met anybody like me before. Yeah right!

They are so charming, that you nearly believe them, even though you know every word that comes out of their mouths is a lie.

Two words best describes this person. Fake and heartless. They only care about themselves. They only have one goal and that is who they can use and abuse.

It takes a very strong woman to get away from this type of guy. They can draw you in so quickly, and before you know it, you can be back where you started. They give you mixed signals that can really wreck your head.

I think years of failed relationships had built up in me, that I wasn't going to let him get away with it.

It was like having a relationship with Dr Jekyll and Mr Hyde.

They depend on people and need to feed their ego. They are always searching for fulfilment in their own lives.

They seem to seek someone who is attractive, rich or someone with status.

They give their new partner their undivided attention and can appear 'full on', for a while.

Narcissists seek out the thrill of a new relationship, and then get bored after a few months because they need constant stimulation.

Their words never match their actions. It's 'from the teeth out'.

A sure sign you are with a narcissistic person, is to try say 'no' to them now and again, and see what reaction you get. They will seem irritated, impatient or get angry, and they can't accept what you're telling them.

They want everybody's world to revolve around them and they don't care for people who are on the receiving end. If it all seems too good to be true, then it most likely is.

When my friend married a Narcissist, I could see things very clearly 'from the outside looking in'.

My friend looked like a model. She had an excellent job with great salary. She was the perfect 'trophy wife'. This was right up his street. It gave him the attention and ego boost he craved.

When I was in their company, he came across as arrogant and would belittle my friend. He was so full of his own self-importance.

He was always boosting about what deals he was making and how much he had made. Of course he only spoke in thousands of pounds. If a conversation was diverted away from him, he had a knack of reining it back to him.

There were rumours of him cheating, but my friend just seemed to block it out. She didn't want to know.

Because I had already been in this type of relationship previously, I was so aware of what was happening. Even though my relationship with Mr Narcissist only lasted months.

I felt my friend had rushed into marriage. Within six months of meeting, they were married. She was mostly the breadwinner. He never seemed to work. She was from a wealthy family. I sometimes wondered if it was her wealth that drew him to her.

She would confide in me, "John's not great at listening. He finds it difficult when I try to tell him something that has upset me."

Great recipe for good marriage. No communication. No empathy. No compassion.

Doesn't want to know!

In most cases, Mr Narcissist has trouble committing. But when he does, it's to his benefit, either financially, for fame or power. It is never for love.

They never seem to get sad. It comes out as rage. It's usually one extreme or the other.

What a Narcissist really wants is the opposite to an emotional, empathetic, compassionate relationship. In other words, it's not a relationship they want.

The bottom line is what a Narcissist truly wants, is a one-way relationship with a detached 'housemate' focused totally on them. This is not a relationship.

Chapter 4
Mr Womaniser

We all know the last one to find out if your partner is cheating on you is you.

Some men, if given the chance, will have several sexual partners.

I can spot a Womaniser when he walks into a room. You can see him scaling the room (with an 'All Eyes On Me Look'). Checking out any females that might make that 'eye contact'.

I have seen men kissing their partners while glancing over their shoulder to see what else is available.

Body language tells a lot.

If your partner is giving you full eye contact and you have his undivided attention, this is a good sign. Touching is another positive. I don't mean wrapped around each other, but just the odd touch to let your partner know they are there. This should be natural and not forced.

Womanisers are very calculating and are always thinking of their next conquest.

I remember at the beginning when I met Mr Womaniser. He was so attractive and charming. I couldn't believe my luck. A month into the relationship we were supposed to be meeting up. He phoned me to say he didn't feel well and he was going to have an early night. I decided to go out with my friends. When we entered the pub, I looked towards the dancefloor and there was 'Casanova' boogieing away with this gorgeous girl. My friends and I went on the dancefloor. Dancing away as if we didn't see him. I near wet myself when I saw him shooting off the dancefloor like a rocket. I followed him and said, "I take it you are feeling a lot better now?"

His face was as white as snow from the shock of seeing me. He couldn't even hide it. He stammered and said, "After couple of hours sleep I felt a lot better. I think it's stress of work."

I just thought, you are such a bad lair.

I had heard, when I started seeing him, that he had a reputation. 'No smoke without fire'. Stupidly, I continued seeing him, but of course a very clear pattern was beginning to emerge.

There was another night where he was going out with his friend. His friend was seeing my friend. About one o'clock in the morning my friend said, "What about us going over to the bar and see what they are up to?"

When we got into the bar, we spied the two boyos talking to two women, looking very cosy. When we approached them, smiling and saying, "Did you have a good night?" I couldn't believe their reaction. They were furious.

I was so shocked because it was the end of the night. Why did it matter? Looking back now, I wonder if he had a plan for that night and a story to tell me the next day why he didn't get home again.

If it was me, I would have been glad to see him. Obviously our love wasn't mutual.

It was so strange because we weren't mad at them. They had no reason to be mad at us unless they were up to 'no good'.

Towards the end of that relationship, it was Mr Womaniser's Christmas staff night out that was the final nail in the coffin of our doomed relationship.

He didn't arrive home until seven am. When he came into the bedroom, he was so full of this 'story,' how there had been a fight and ambulances were called and the police were involved. The reason he was so late home was because the police were questioning them.

I felt something just didn't add up.

I rang the same bar the following day. A female answered. I explained that my partner left his coat behind because of the fight that had broken out previous night. There was silence.

She said, "There was no fight last night."

I said, "Are you sure?"

She said, "I was here all night, there was definitely no fight."

I said, "Sorry to have bothered you. My partner obviously has told me a huge whopper."

He started laughing when I told him he had been caught out. I think he was so shocked that he had been found out. He knew I was no fool.

I told him what about all the lies that I don't know about. He was still laughing. Then he tried to defend himself with another lie. The whole thing was a joke to him.

I packed my bags and left.

I remember once he told me a lie about his age, he was twenty-eight at the time, but he knocked two years off. I couldn't get my head around this. What difference would two years make. It all makes sense now. If he would lie about that, then he would lie about anything. Time proved that to be right.

It's a losing battle with a guy like this. They get a kick out of the thrill of not getting caught.

A lot of womanisers are big into gift buying flowers, etc. That always represented to me a man with a guilty conscience. Special occasions maybe, but constantly is like a smoke screen for something they are guilty of.

Nowadays women have lots of opportunities to find out if someone is cheating.

I know a man who was caught with two phones by his wife. When she checked the second phone she found in his drawer, there were texts to other women. She approached him. Why had he two phones? He made up some excuse that he had just got a second one for his business. Then when she asked him why he had texts from other women, he accused her of being devious but she didn't trust him.

It's funny the way they can turn the situation around to you and point out your faults.

When she went onto their computer, he had forgot to log off. There were intimate messages from a woman to her husband.

She bit her tongue. When he went to bed early that night, she checked his phone, and low and behold, he had been sexting this woman for six months.

She phoned her up and said, "Do realise you are having an affair with my husband?"

She denied she ever knew anything, but she could tell the woman was lying.

The next morning when the man woke up, she had all his bags packed and told him to leave. He turned everything around saying the woman was hounding him.

But she told him she had read all the emails and sexts.

I commended this girl on her strength and not giving him a second chance. Not many women have that courage, especially when she had three children.

She told me afterwards she felt he had stuck a knife in her heart.

Anybody that knew this couple were so shocked. They were the last couple anyone would have thought that an affair would have broken up their marriage.

I don't believe anybody can 'rest on their laurels'. It could happen to anyone. You know when your partner is cheating, I think, you get that gut instinct, but it's whether or not you want to find the truth.

I know a few couples that have 'open relationships'. That's alright if it's what both partners want.

In some cases, there are women who turn a blind eye to their partners' philandering. Maybe they can't bear to leave them. Or pride has taken over and they don't want to be known as the woman whose husband has cheated.

There is no shame on any woman whose husband has cheated. The shame is on him.

I would say there are very few women who go through life without having been cheated on at least once.

'Once a Cheater Always a Cheater?'

Chapter 5
Mr Addictive

From an early age, I experienced an addictive personality in the form of my father.

Addiction can come in the form of:

- Alcohol
- Drugs
- Prescription drugs
- Food
- Gambling
- Sex
- Work
- Sport

It actually became quite useful as I got older, in that I could spot an alcoholic/gambler etc. a mile off.

Whenever I met a guy, I watched him like a 'hawk', to see how much they drank. It became obsessive for me because of what I experienced. The fear of living with someone with an addiction again terrified me. Once in a lifetime was enough for me. I could not face it again. If they were always drunk when I would meet up with them, then I would 'run for the hills.'

Meeting a 'potential' alcoholic is a tricky one. They may be able to 'hold' their drink better than others. Some people can drink huge amounts and they would never show any outward signs.

My father was an alcoholic for years before my mother knew, by that stage he was so far in the grips of alcohol and gambling that the only way forward was 'rock bottom'.

My mother became the sole provider and sole parent.

Life with an alcoholic or substance abuse user can mean a life with disasters, infidelity, abuse, rape, medical emergencies, accidents, court visits and jail.

You become the 'messenger', when they don't turn up to their work or family gatherings.

Your life becomes consumed with this disease, and you cut yourself off from friends and family, because you don't know when they will come home and how bad they will be.

Some alcoholics think they can 'control' their drinking, but eventually it gets out of control. Some would say they can't even have one drink because they just don't know when to stop.

To watch a loved one destroy their life and let alcohol, etc. take over their lives is heart-breaking.

People on the outside looking in can see the addict's life crashing down around them and feel so helpless. Eventually most women find they have to put themselves and their kids first, when all the promises that have been made to them have been broken time and time again. The inevitable happens and they have to do 'tough love', to break free.

I met a guy once who seemed to be more interested in 'holding up the bar' than taking me for a meal or spending quality time with me.

If this is happening at the beginning of the relationship, then there is little chance of things changing. The beginning of any relationship should be the best time and most exciting, not unhappy and miserable.

If you are always seeming to be dragging your partner away from the bar in the early hours, then you need to ask yourself, "Is this the way you want your future to be?"

I know some women that were happy to do this, and then they got married and had kids with this person. Things didn't change.

Alcohol and gambling sometimes go 'hand in hand'. In my experience, my mother ended up paying for everything because my father never had any money. You can become a crutch for that person. 'Tough love' is very hard to incorporate when you love someone or have children with them.

Some women take on the 'carer' role, but this is a no-win situation. It will always be a one-way relationship and you may never find that fulfilling relationship.

Alcoholics are very cunning and they can promise you they will change. But very few do. They can lie, cheat, and steal. It's deciding whether to give up your own life to help them and then you may never have a life!

Sometimes alcoholics do not remember what emotional and physical abuse they have caused. In some cases, they drink to block out emotional pain. It's a vicious cycle. When they begin to become sober, they need more alcohol to block everything out.

There are a few men that I know, that when they are drinking, everybody avoids them like the plague. As soon as their personality begins to change, everybody watches what they say.

Any comment could send them into a rage. When you are in a relationship and you live with that person, you can't walk away so easily.

Treading on eggshells in case an argument ensues. It's like having a child. You are more like the carer than a partner.

The dynamics of the relationship change. It becomes one sided.

They can't contribute to this relationship emotionally and in most cases financially.

No matter which addiction has taken over your lives, this person cannot give their 100% to the relationship. Something has to come to the wall. Therefore, there is very little room and time left for their partner.

Alcoholics can become violent.

I remember watching a programme about men that get out of their mind drunk, during football season. The rise in domestic violence during this time is huge. Women were terrified, especially if their partners' team lost. They know what was in front of them. Alcohol fuelled violence. It's so sad to think that this is what is happening in some homes, I'm sure all over the world.

In a lot of cases, in these homes, there is no food in the cupboards, no heating and no clothing for the kids. Some women have no family or friends to turn to.

Mentally and physically, the carer suffers.

In rare cases, alcoholics can be highly functioning. Able to carry on working, etc.

Some alcoholics are house drinkers.

They can blame their drinking on stress or maybe they have had to deal with a death recently. There will always be an excuse so they can continue drinking.

Some alcoholics don't become sober until they have been told they have cirrhosis of the liver, or they have been told by their doctor they have so many months to live.

Alcoholics live in denial that they have problem with alcohol. Alcohol will be their number one priority, and when they aren't drinking, they are thinking when will they get the next one.

When you're living a 'crazy life' with an alcoholic, it's very difficult, because you are trying to keep your relationship/family intact, and as 'normal' as you possibly can.

As a child I spent most of my life by the window, watching and waiting for my father to return. Hoping and praying that day would be different from all the others. My mother may have thought 'I'm staying for the children'. It was no life. From my perspective it was a life of fear and my childhood was taken away and consumed with a parent who was addicted to alcohol and prescription drugs.

Sometimes alcoholism can begin by going for a drink after work.

I have seen it over and over, women trying to get their men home from the pub.

I know a woman whose husband had a very highly paid job. They had a very comfortable life, which included a couple of holidays a year. For years he was drinking and gambling before she knew he got into debt and they nearly lost their home. He began to steal to pay for his addictions and consequently lost his job. This just doesn't happen over-night. It could take years before life begins to crumble.

I heard of another woman who paid for her husband's debts, but of course that didn't stop him from drinking/gambling. She was just enabling him. He didn't want to change. You can bring the horse to the water but you can't make it drink.

The addict has to want to do it for themselves first and foremost.

You can't 'save' everybody.

Chapter 6
Mr Couch Potato

Sloth is one of the seven deadly sins. If you are unfortunate enough to have a partner such as this, you have my sympathy.

The lazy man is more common that you think.

A person who has no motivation in life but to sit in front of the television, on their back side, day in, day out. Even if they do work full-time, it's no excuse.

As each month passes, he's beginning to look more like 'Jabba the Hutt' than the man you first met.

Of course, if us women do everything in the home, then they will sit back and let us.

Millions of women work full-time work and come home and do another day's work, cooking, cleaning, kid's homework, and laundry.

If you are also that type of person, then maybe that type of relationship will suit you.

Can you imagine being in a relationship with someone who is a lazy sow and does not contribute physically or emotionally to the home, or to their children?

I am aware that this does happen. I have known women who have had children to this type of man. If men don't contribute after your first child, it sure isn't going to change after the second one. If someone is living with a couch potato, you would be better off being a single parent, because that's the role you're living anyway. I have heard women regretting having so many kids to someone who doesn't help in the home in any way, shape or form. Let's face it, if they aren't contributing, financially by working, helping in the home and being there emotionally for you, and the children, what have you got to lose?

I believe in positive role models and a single parent can provide enough love for both parents. A negative role model only highlights the type of person you don't want your children to be. The same is for a person who is verbally abusive or hits their partner. If children are witnessing 'types' of behaviour, they may think, this is the way to live my life, and this is the way to treat women.

A person told me she was visiting a relative and their little boy told his mummy to 'shut up'. When his father told him not to speak to his mother like that, the little boys reply was, "But that's what you say to mummy".

Living with a person who does 'nothing' all day. There is no positive role model for children to see.

Even if children are not in the equation. Why would any woman want to be a man's 'doormat'?

Some men like to be 'mothered'. They are perfectly happy to let you do everything. These men usually have been spoilt by the mothers and they think a woman's place is in the home.

I can understand women who give in so many times because they are tired of nagging men into helping.

Some excuses are, 'I can't do it as well as you and you complain anyway.'

Face reality. You are aiding a man who has no respect or love for the person whom he is supposed to love.

You have to ask yourself, will this man ever fulfil all my needs in life? It's a form of 'me, myself and I.' Having their cake and eating it.

What you accept in this type of relationship is what you are going to get from it.

There are some women who are in this relationship for years. Who have eventually left because their partner never changed. It was like a weight lifted from them. Making the decision to leave is the hardest.

If you put up with being treated like a doormat, then some people will happily take advantage.

I hear some women cry, 'but I love him.' What's to love from someone who constantly takes and never gives anything positive in return?

Have you accepted this is your role in life? Eventually you will be totally depleted and unfulfilled emotionally. No relationship could sustain that. Resentment and anger will build up over a period of time until you eventually realise that enough is enough.

I have heard women say, 'I should have left him earlier.' In most cases, women feel their partner will eventually change over time.

Life's too short to be wasting your time on a 'time waster'. Your time is precious, take respect back. If you have no self-worth or respect for yourself, why is anyone else going to bother?

I have been in a few relationships similar to this, and also been on the 'outside looking in'.

Hindsight can be a reality check and an eye-opener. When you come out the other side, you think to yourself, 'what was I thinking'?

If you have just started down the road in your relationship and he never offers to help you out in the house, well, you are living under the same roof, then he should be contributing someway in the housework, gardening, cooking, etc.

If it's an equal relationship, then he should be equally helping out.

If you mention bed, I'm sure there would be no hesitation in that department.

Mothers have a lot to answer for.

I remember my cousin telling me when her son was three years old he said to his daddy while he was hoovering. 'Why are you doing that, Daddy? That is mummy's job.' Unbelievable! But her husband is the absolute antithesis of couch potato so we have no idea where he got it from. Probably television.

Years ago men got away without helping in the home, because they had full-time jobs. Because women stayed at home, men just expected women to cook, clean, change nappies and do the shopping.

Nowadays, we do have a lot of house-husbands because the woman is earning more than the man. In other cases, the man can't find a job, so it makes sense for him to stay home to mind the kids and look after the house.

Men love praise. So if my husband helps me in the house, even though he lives there too, I always let him know he's a great help to me. Therefore, it encourages him to do more. There's a method in my madness.

Some men control their wives by demanding their wives do everything. These women just get on with it because they don't have a choice if their husband is a bully. It's easier to keep the peace.

Some men have been lazy all their lives and they don't know any different.

I know men that have been mollycoddled by their mothers and never had to lift a finger. From they have got married, their wives have made them help out because they couldn't do it all on their own.

I remember buying a wicker basket for our en suite for dirty laundry. For years I couldn't get my husband to put his dirty washing into this basket instead of the floor.

Eventually I gave up. I decided to use the basket for clean towels. Two days later, I went to take a clean towel and there was a load of dirty washing on top of the clean towels. I thought he has done that on badness. When I approached him, he starting laughing. I said I have been trying to get you to do that for two years and when I use it for clean towels, you dump dirty washing into it. He couldn't believe what he had done. Unbelievable!

Some men find it hard to get motivated.

My husband fills the dishwasher and I empty it. We are both clear as to whose job is what.

Lazy men at home are usually lazy when it comes to anything to do with their relationship. They forget birthday gifts and Christmas. They just trudge through their life with no ambition and no motivation.

Lazy about their personal hygiene and appearance is the worst.

Some men remain boys throughout their life and never grow up. You become their mother instead of their wife.

If he cares about you and wants you to be happy, he will help you out in the home if it makes you happy and eases your stress.

If you are exhausted and unhappy because you are constantly trying to catch up on housework, would he not eventually realise that an unhappy wife is an unhappy husband in the bedroom department?

I remember hearing a woman who told her husband the electric was off when he came home from work, thinking he won't have any excuses now not to help her out. When she turned around to speak to him, he was asleep on the couch. Some women have the patience of Job.

'Where's my clean shirt?'

'I presumed it wasn't dirty when it wasn't in the laundry basket.'

Be the Captain of your own ship and don't be nobody's fool.

Chapter 7
Mr Miser

There's a difference between being wise and thrifty with your money and being a 'miser'. With some men, it's an obsession with money.

Money can be the source of many an argument in relationships. But arguments with someone who won't spend money, when they can well afford it is a whole different story.

Especially if they earn more than you and still expect bills to be split 50/50.

Sometimes the more money they have, the more they want.

I have to admit, I love getting a bargain, especially on eBay, and I get such a thrill going into a second-hand shop and picking up an antique for a few quid. It can be addictive when you know you have got something in the sale that has been slashed from £100 to £20. I love it when people say that must have cost you a fortune and I tell them it did, but I got it in a sale for next to nothing. I believe in buying gifts for friends and family, to show my appreciation for someone who has helped me out in some way. As the saying goes, 'when you are kind with your money, it comes back twofold.'

Even though I have friends that earn way more than me, I still believe in buying gifts for them, when they have been kind to me. Even though I don't earn anywhere near the same as them.

Mr Miser is on a different planet altogether. He does not believe in spending unnecessarily.

Mr Miser very rarely buys presents. Sometimes they will use the excuse of not knowing what to buy you, and if he does, it's something very cheap and not practical.

Living with them is such a misery. Heating rarely on in winter. Complains about price of food and presents. Always asking the price of groceries/clothes you have bought.

Watching every penny is a control thing and can be used in a relationship to curtail women's choices and spending. You can't go out with friends for coffee or a meal, or you can't join membership classes, because all these things are eating up too much money.

Weddings are another nightmare. Mr Miser doesn't go to weddings because he has to buy a wedding present, new suit, and in some cases has to pay for night in hotel. It's just too stressful for them, so they tell you to go ahead. How embarrassing, another episode where their partner has to make up excuses for them.

There's a miser in every family. The whole family go out for a celebratory meal. Then Mr Scrooge spoils it all, by patting his trouser pocket and counting out what he owes in change.

It can be very embarrassing when you go out with friends, which rarely happens. He's always last to buy a round. If it's a meal out, he checks the cost of our meal and gives the money, down to last penny.

When I have ever been out for a meal with friends, some people have a starter and some have dessert. The bill is always split equally. In some cases, people who order a bottle of wine pay for it. Other than that, a few pound here and there doesn't make a difference, when you know the people you are eating out with are genuine friends. Most people will offer to pay extra if they have had full three-course meal. You always tip of course. Misers don't believe in tipping.

Women who I know that have 'tight' husbands have kept their jobs on after kids were born, so they didn't have to beg for money if they need to buy a top, or kids needed new shoes etc. It just saves a lot of hassle and arguments. As one friend told me, you have to pick your arguments, otherwise your marriage becomes just one great big battle.

It's worse when he earns more money than you and he still insists on splitting the bills, and thinks he's doing you a favour.

One of my friends was out with her new boyfriend and he insisted on going to a posh restaurant. She thought he must be treating me.

At the end of the meal he realised he had forgotten his wallet. She was so embarrassed that she ended up paying about £80 for it. Not a bit of wonder he was knocking the drinks down. She thought he'll pay me back when we get home. Nope, not a chance. Even though he had a great-paying job. Obviously she broke off the relationship when his true colours began to show. What a cheap skate!

Very few of us were born with a silver spoon in our mouths. We know what it's like when you go through periods of having very little disposable cash. But some men stay in a time warp where they think they are still poor, and feel no shame in ripping their partner's friends and family off, through pure greed. They are being tight at somebody else's expense and it doesn't seem to bother them.

The wealthy men are the worst, and they won't spend a penny more than they have to.

Everybody loves to go for a nice meal. It's chill-out time and relaxation. But going for a meal with scrooge is beyond relaxing, because you are wondering has he taken his wallet with him this time.

Having to live your whole life with someone like this would be like a living hell.

A couple of women I know that have scrooges for husbands are out earning their own money. Because the stress of asking husbands when they needed something was too much to bear.

Especially self-made men, they believe that penny pinching has got them financially where they are now, and they feel if they rest on their laurels, they will be right back where they started, before they become rich.

I have known men who I have shared a taxi with and got out of the car without paying, and because I was last one dropped off, the bill was left for me to pay.

Long term, a relationship with Mr Scrooge will leave you financially embarrassed. It's nice in the beginning of a relationship when a man pays for meals, gifts, etc. But I believe in going 'Dutch'. Start as you mean to go on. You wouldn't want him to expect you to pay for everything and vice versa. If you find that you are always 'forking out' and he never pays, well that's not a good start.

In my experience 'men with money' find it hard to part with it. Obviously that's not true in all cases. On the other hand, some men try to buy their women, but that's a whole other story.

Sometimes, when it's not birthdays or Christmas, etc. it's nice to be thought of. Random treats don't have to be expensive, it could just be a bar of chocolate or your favourite magazine.

A few times, I went out with men for a meal and they have sat back and let me pay. Let me tell you 'once bitten twice shy'. There wasn't a second meeting.

I remember booking a holiday abroad with an ex-boyfriend. He told me to book somewhere hot. He would leave it up to me to decide where. I paid for the holiday and he told me he would pay me back. Holiday came and went, and twenty-five years later, I am still waiting on the money. One thing is for sure, I never booked, nor paid for anybody's holiday ever again. That was one sorry lesson I learnt.

If you marry a Mr Miser, no need to wreck your brains and guess who will be footing all the bills. What a life! What a relationship!

Having a weekend away is an investment into your relationship, rather than both of you becoming two people who share the same roof.

In this economic climate, we have all learned to tighten the purse strings. There is nothing wrong now and again for a treat to give you an emotional lift. Sometimes we can't always afford a meal out, but we can compromise and go out for morning coffee or breakfast. It's all about time out with the love of your life and a change of scenery. Change is as good as a rest.

Nothing wrong with 'un petit achat'. It goes a long way towards keeping your marriage 'on track'. We all have tiny potholes in our relationships. As long as they don't amalgamate into one huge sink hole.

It's especially hard in a relationship if he's the frugal one and you're not. Let's face it, it's not good if you're the type that has more money outgoing than incoming. Happy medium is the key.

If your partner decides that you don't need holidays because it costs too much and you <u>can</u> afford it, then it could be a case of either he's a hermit or is obsessed with not spending money. It has been known that people who make their first million don't like to spend because they are aiming for the second million.

If frugality is at its extreme and taking over your relationship, then it's time to re-evaluate. Maybe they are OCD about money. Then you need to decide if you can you live a lifetime like this.

Mr Miser's birthdays/Christmas gifts are the best – NOT.

I remember getting set of mugs with mug tree. Bless! and a £10.00 voucher. I nearly wet myself. What the heck would you get with £10? I thought to myself the only mug here is me.

Even twenty years ago you might have got two pairs of socks or pants. I suppose he thought he was pushing the boat out by buying two gifts. I lost the will to live. He wouldn't have spent Christmas.

I tried to remind him 'there are no pockets in a shroud.'

He would have sold his granny if he thought he was going to make a few quid.

Some men who have money but just won't spend it, are just plain greedy. Money becomes their god.

If money is priority over you and your relationship in the early stages, then you need to ask yourself, do you think it's going to get any better in the future? The chances are very slim. If he knows it's making you unhappy and he doesn't change, it's time to re-evaluate.

Chapter 8
Mr Mummy's Boy

You've heard it said, 'if a man is good to his mother, then he will be good to his wife'. A mummy's boy is the extreme of this.

In my experience, some of the men I had relationships with did not treat me the same as they treated their mother. Some people might say, 'Well, maybe it was you'. After the relationship ended, I heard from another one of their exes, that they treated them the same way. It was a relief. For months or years, I would have thought it was my fault or my personality that triggered the negative side of their personality. They will constantly tell you it was your fault.

I have heard of this 'study' and that 'research' that men who are good to their mothers will treat their wives the same. I think it's more complicated than that. Well in my experience anyway, it's not as 'cut and dried'.

My husband is an only boy, but thankfully not a mummy's boy. They had a very good relationship before she took dementia. He is respectful to his mother, but they never lived in each other's pockets. I believe it was a very healthy relationship. He might not always have agreed with her, but they never argued. In my eyes, it was exactly how a mother and son should be. He would do anything for his mother, but he had his own life, and she was respectful of that. He has always been there for her and she knew she could rely on him.

It's worse if your partner/husband tells his mother everything, especially if you both have had an argument.

I remember my ex's mother coming over one day and saying to us, "Is everything ok now?"

I had no idea what she was talking about. I asked him, "What did she mean?"

He said, "She knew I wasn't in good form the other day when we had the argument and she kept quizzing me about our relationship. I just said we had a small tiff."

As you can imagine, I was livid. I told him from now on put a happy face on when you go to visit your mother.

She would phone constantly, for him to do this and that for her. It was like a full-time job attending to her. So I told him, I would do certain messages for her to ease burden on him. She stopped giving so many orders because she didn't want me getting involved, and didn't have much time for me.

I understood she was lonely, but his siblings sat back and did nothing while he done it all.

It's bound to affect any relationship; you have to find a balance. It takes a while for some mothers to realise that their sons do have a life, especially if kids come along. They have to cut the apron strings some time.

Okay, I have to admit it's nice to see a man who has respect for his mother and treats her well. But Mummy's boys go overboard.

One of my experiences of a man who treated his mother extremely well, is that he left nothing for me. He treated me the opposite to her, which is quite puzzling. I thought I was on to a winner with him, but sadly that didn't materialise. Being with him was like being with a 'dry drunk'. I would have classed him as a mummy's boy, but it was like the film *Sleeping With the Enemy*. He was the nightmare from hell.

Mummy's boys get calls from their mothers while they are supposed to be spending time with you.

I know women who have had to curb their husbands from seeing their mothers so much, because it was affecting their relationship. Especially if she puts them in a bad mood, and then he carries it home to you. That's never going to work.

Some 'monster-in-laws' can be very controlling and can't accept that their son has left them for another woman, all be it, his wife. HA!

I'm a mother of two boys, so I can understand a tiny little bit how that must feel.

It's worse if you meet these men, and they are over thirty, and are still living with their mother. As long as you know, if you decide to take over their role, you will have to pick up were his mother left off.

I knew of one girl who met a new boyfriend's mother on a second date. What a shocker!

Can you imagine being married to this type of man and his mother coming in, dictating what curtains, tiles, etc. to put into your new house? I know one girl who got up one morning drew the curtains to find her mother-in-law actually planting the plants and flowers that she wanted in their garden. Could you imagine being in conflict with someone who is continually a third wheel in your relationship?

You don't want to be saying years down the line, 'Well, there were three people in this relationship.'

There's no competing, he's already mummy's boy, and he's known her longer than he has you.

I remember once my ex's mother called me by another girl's name. Okay, it may have been a slip of the tongue, but when she infuriatingly continued to call me this name, it made me so angry, so I called her by the wrong surname, she was so angry. I didn't care, because I finished the relationship soon after.

If you're having a romantic meal out and phone keeps ringing, it can be so infuriating. It's virtually impossible to break this mother-and-son bond. You're fighting a losing battle. Unless you and him decide to move a 100 miles away. Ha!

Another thing that bugged me was, "Mummy says it would be better, etc. etc." I used to think, 'Do you not have a mind of your own?'

Turning up un-announced on a Friday evening when you have just sat down to a glass of wine after a stressful working week. Breakfast dishes still in the sink. Especially when I was on my own then, she would start dictating that house could do with a lick of paint. Future mothers-in-law know exactly which buttons to press. So I started to agree with everything she said. I know it annoyed her, that's why I did it. Then when I would tell my partner what she said, he would always be on her side, and would say 'she means well.' Grrrrrrrrrrrrrrr!

The worst thing was when he would invite her round for Sunday dinner, and she would comment that her daughter cooks a lovely roast. That was the first and last invite.

There's only so much one person can take, especially when it's two against one.

Then I realised no wonder he was in his thirties and still living at home. That was a dead giveaway.

No matter how many recipes you get from his mother, he will tell you it's just not the same as his mother's cooking/baking.

It's heart breaking when he is always trying to please his mother and sometimes fails, but continues to yearn for that compliment or reassurance that he has been a good son. He will spend his life trying to please her.

Sometimes when a man's father has died young, or left the mother, then her son has become the substitute husband or father to his siblings.

A Mummy's boy always gets everything done for him. From his washing to his cooking.

In some cases, their mother has been a distant nag and very hard to please.

You always feel as if you're the 'blow in' and sometimes you feel as if it's a losing battle.

Mummy's boys feel as if they have to confide everything to their mothers because that's what they did before you were on 'the scene'. She was his sole confidante.

She is afraid of her life and that you are going to take him away, if you haven't already.

She 'nit picks' constantly and questions everything you do and the decisions you make. If your own mother says something, it doesn't get under your skin the way it can with your mother-in-law.

When she's around, your other half is a different person. He turns into this little puppy dog and just answers her beck and call.

He still seeks that reassurance he has always needed from his childhood.

Only boys can be the 'blue eyed'. These can be the worse types of mummy's boys. Their mothers can make you feel as if you are having an affair. Because you are taking their son away from them.

Mothers and their sons!

Chapter 9
Mr Passive Aggressive

Passive-aggressive men don't like confrontation. It is easier for them to hold anger and resentment internally, than to say to their partner, "I was really hurt by what you said or did." They are afraid of conflict, so they feel it's better to avoid it.

They are very calculated in their thinking. Especially when they are not happy with a decision or action their partner has made. Sometimes they will put on a display that everything's okay, but underneath, they are full of rage and resentment. They can be so discreet to your face, but behind your back, they are ridiculing you.

They can wind you up by not doing things around the house that they usually do, and can withhold affection and intimacy, just to get their revenge. They love sarcasm, and can make a joke with a jag.

They sometimes give you the silent treatment, that could last days or weeks.

I remember when I was living with my parents, I knew when my father wasn't happy with me. He just stopped speaking to me for at least three or four days. I just got the cold shoulder. I would never find out the reason why he was actually not speaking to me. When he would sleep on the couch, I knew my poor mother was getting the silent treatment. The atmosphere in the house was terrible. I never realised he was passive aggressive until recently. When I would say something to him that he didn't like, he would go to my mother and tell her. He would play the victim. He had told her a completely different story. He had turned the whole thing around. My mother would say how hurt he was and that he's a very sensitive man. When she told me he was crying, I thought, 'now that deserves an Oscar'. He was very manipulative but charming, and came across as very plausible. He was also very intelligent. I don't ever remember my parents arguing, except when he was drinking. He would just walk away, so there was never much communication in their relationship that I could see. Maybe that's why I have a thing about talking over the smallest of issues before they turn into one huge mountain of trouble.

I think the reason my parents' marriage lasted so long was because my mother was so easy going, and decided to let him get on with whatever way he wanted to behave. I remember her asking him what was bothering him and if she had done something to annoy him. He just walked out of the room, got into the car and left. I can still visualise my mother rolling her eyes and clenching her teeth in frustration.

Passive Aggressive usually find a relationship with someone who has low self-esteem.

Passive-aggressive men never forget any past hurts that have been done to them. They make very unreliable partners. They can also be very heartless and cruel. Especially if you are sick, they carry on with life as if nothing is wrong. I don't think they have the empathy gene. But when the tables are turned, well that's a different story. The whole world knows they are sick and they expect everybody to rally round. They like being in control of other people.

I remember at birthdays and Christmases; it was never about what my father was buying me, but what I was going to buy him. He was very good at dropping hints about what gifts he would like to receive. I remember feeling really guilty one year, but as I got older, I realised he wasn't too worried about getting me anything. Eventually he realised we weren't falling for it and he give up hinting.

They are very immature and never seem to grow up. It's like a little child, 'what am I getting for my birthday?' 'What are you doing for me?' A child rarely thinks what can I do for you?

In my experience, passive-aggressive men are very cold, calculated people. Your life revolves around them and their behaviour. It is like walking on eggshells and you're constantly trying to humour them.

At the beginning of the relationship, you feel that you are to blame for them feeling so low and you do feel guilty. As time goes by, and you have tried every avenue to help these people, you realise that there is only so much you can do. It can be a tough battle.

Passive-aggressive men cannot deal with people who are needy. They don't know how to relate in situations where empathy is needed.

All the qualities that are needed in a relationship, these men can be lacking. You never get to the crux of any problem because they won't actually sit you down and talk about what they are not happy with.

It can be so frustrating in a relationship like this. They can be very petty over the slightest thing they didn't agree with.

It's a subtle underlying and discreet form of abuse.

You know something is up, but when you ask them, they are in denial and make you think you are going crazy.

When they are in this mode, they are controlling your mind in a way, because you know something is wrong, but you can't get to the root of it.

Problems can build up for years, and nothing ever gets resolved. They just carry on through life, building up these hidden resentments, and their partners never fully know how they have been feeling.

A relationship cannot reach its full potential with a Passive Aggressive, because you never fully know what they are thinking or feeling. So there will always be an invisible wall. You know and can feel that they aren't one hundred percent happy, but you can't make them talk.

With the passive aggressive, you are living under their rules of manipulation and game playing. It's about 'me, myself and I'.

Being a partner of a passive aggressive is so unpredictable. It can take a long time to figure them out. When you are getting the silent treatment, you have no control over them, and no matter what you do, to try and break down the wall of silence, they are a hard nut to crack. They will start speaking to you when they decide if ever.

They are very poor communicators and expect their partners to read their minds and know why they have stopped speaking, etc.

They may let you decide where to go or what to do, and then give you the silent treatment because they aren't happy with what you decided.

It is a relationship of constant analysing and trying to resolve. Women in relationships with passive-aggressive men never fully get to know the true person because so much is hidden under their mask.

Chapter 10
Mr Asperger

If you have ever watched *Big Bang Theory* then you will know Sheldon Cooper as one of the characters from the show. He epitomises Autism.

Children and adults with autism have difficulty connecting with other people on a social and emotional level.

I have a son who reminds me of Sheldon, even though he's only six. He has autism also, but thankfully he has more compassion and affection than Sheldon has. One of my relations, I would say has autism also, he is a man of few words and never liked making eye contact and is very odd in his ways.

I believe we are all on the spectrum of autism, obviously at different levels.

I have had a relationship with someone with autism, but at the time I just thought he was very eccentric. When I look back now, I can see he had all the traits. I did find him quite 'wooden' and predictable. I would also say that he wasn't an affectionate person. I know a lot of men and women who aren't 'huggers'. He certainly wasn't. I was more a friend to him than a girlfriend. He thrived on routine. Got up at 7.30 am. Lunch at one. Tea at six. Television off at 10.15 to be in bed for 10.30.

Routine, routine, routine.

Like Sheldon, he had certain meals on certain days. Monday was chicken, Tuesday was pasta, Wednesday was Chinese, etc. etc.

I found myself fascinated by him. I knew from early on there definitely was no chemistry.

He found it hard to make full eye contact when he was speaking to me. He would look down or past me. He had little to no social skills. When I use to wind him up, he never got the fact that I was joking with him, and he took everything literally.

He went to the gym every day after his tea. Football was Saturday.

Sometimes you don't realise how great their routine is until you live with them. And a lot of men with Asperger's can and do get married.

Their life is based on routine, even if their child was sick, they still went to see their friends or got to football practice or gym. Nothing will detract them from their routine.

I know I have traits of autism in me, and so does my husband, but thankfully they are mild.

When I was young I wouldn't have said boo to a goose. I was as odd as two left feet. My husband reminds me how much I've made up for it now. Whereas he's quite shy. I call him the 'quiet man'.

If I said to my husband, I need to go into town, would you drop me of at the chemist? No problem.

When I come out of the shop and ask him to go to another shop, he cannot deal with this. Even though he has no other plans, he says he needs to be prepared where he's going. The first time that happened I laughed. I said what do you need to be prepared about? You're just dropping me off, I'm not asking you to go in. Then I realised that was one of his pet peeves. He needs to know in advance what's happening.

I suppose we all have our own pet peeves.

One of my old work colleagues is married to someone who I would say has autism but has never been diagnosed. She told me once she had another friend around to visit, her husband walked in the room when the friend was discussing dieting. Her husband pipes up, "Well if you would stay away from the buns you would lose weight a bit quicker." His wife nearly died.

No Filter!

Whatever they think, it just comes out with no apology. My friend also said that he told his boss one day if you weren't so stingy with your pay, I would work a bit harder. The boss just ignored it. I would say everybody knows someone like that, and conclude that is just the way they are. They seem to get away with it.

When I have been in his company, he talks about topics he likes to talk about. When someone changes the subject, he will start talking about another topic that nobody else is interested in.

I remember my friend on her wedding day. I met her in the toilets during the reception. She was such an unhappy bride. Maybe she realised she had made a mistake, but I couldn't ask her what was wrong, unless she volunteered how she felt. I just talked away.

In saying all that, twenty odd years later and four kids, she's still with him. So it can't be all bad. I would say she has adopted to his ways and personality.

In contrast, I know a marriage that didn't last, because the husband's ways were so extreme, that he was too challenging to live with.

People with Asperger's don't get sarcasm. Some find it hard to understand jokes, and some have never known what it's like to have a 'good belly laugh'. They can come across as very serious people.

On a positive note, they are highly intelligent and they will always tell you the truth. Don't ever ask them 'is my bum big in this?'

They can take things literally and get the wrong end of the stick.

Sometimes being married to someone with Asperger's, you find yourself going to events like weddings etc. on your own. They can find large groups of people overwhelming. Some women find it very difficult to adopt to their 'ways'. If you have kids, you can feel as if you are a single parent. They can sometimes 'check out' of parenthood, without even realising they are doing it.

I know in some cases, men with Asperger's can't understand the way their wife is reacting to their lack of emotion in some situations, especially if there has been a death in the family. They think everything should carry on as normal.

At times when you most need your partner, that can be a time when you feel most on your own. We all need emotional support from time to time. They can have very little compassion or empathy.

Some husbands find it hard to change.

When my son was a toddler, he would push me away when I asked him for a hug. Then at times he would hug me for half an hour. From one extreme to the other. I never gave up, and I would grab a quick hug and now he's very affectionate. This took time and patience.

They need their own space much more than most of us.

Some relationships like this can work, but it requires patience and tolerance.

These men find it hard to communicate with their partners and children. In a lot of cases, their children have autism too.

When women have kids, they realise something's up when one of their kids has a bad fall and injury and there is little reaction or empathy from the husband. They can't help it.

They can express their love for their family practically rather than emotionally.

They buy practical gifts because they can see that is what you need, e.g. hoover breaks down, they get you a hoover, etc. If you told them, you won a million on the lotto, there would be no great reaction that most of us would have.

Partners usually find ways around the relationship by accepting the things they cannot change in them and live in a sexless marriage with no affection or emotional support. Some partners may be tempted to have affairs or eventually leave the relationship. The important part of a relationship, where women need to feel loved and wanted, falls apart.

Some people decide better the devil you know and live a lonely life, all be it, under the same roof as their partner.

Chapter 11
Mr Pinocchio

It never ceases to amaze me, that men who are pathological liars, never realise you need a good memory to be a good liar. They eventually get found out.

If I had a penny for every man that lied to me, I would never have to work another day in my life.

Most people have told 'white lies' at some time or another, but some men take lying to a different level. They lie to cover up something they don't want their girlfriend/wife to know about.

Pathological liars just can't help themselves. It seems like a habit and a way of life, they can't break free from. Little lies and big lies. When they are found out, they will always have an explanation ready.

I remember on one first date, this guy had borrowed his father's car because his car was a 'banger'. And so what, we all had a banger at some stage in our lives and were just glad to have four wheels to get us from A to B. As the relationship got more serious, I realised the first car he was driving was different to the next one the following week. When I eventually met his mum and dad, low and behold, his dad drove the same model of car he had met me on our first meeting. Or so I thought.

He told me he was born in 1967 and at the time he was thirty-five. When we went on our first holiday together, I realised by his passport he was actually born in 1965 which made him thirty-seven. It goes beyond all understanding why did two years make a difference to him. Very strange. I could see through it if he was about to turn forty and was knocking a few years off because he couldn't bear the thought of turning forty.

He took me to a seaside apartment he apparently owned. It was beautiful with a balcony and sea view. It was quite sparse looking inside, with no photographs, which I thought a bit strange. A couple of months later, he told me he had sold it. It wasn't until I found out all the other lies that I realised it wasn't his apartment at all. I got talking to a friend of his and I said how lovely my boyfriend's apartment was and I thought he was mad selling it. Well, his face said it all, and he conveniently changed the subject very quickly.

Looking back, he seemed to be living a life that didn't exist, he was living in dream land or a fantasy world. He was trying to be someone he obviously wasn't. He used to always boost about his friends who had yachts and fancy cars. He was great at 'name dropping'. Funny, as time went by I never met any of these friends. But I would have loved to have had a sail on their yacht.

As time went on, anything he told me, I would take with a pinch of salt and I always doubted his word. I thought if he's lying about small things, what else is he lying about?

He would come home at seven in the morning and tell me he couldn't get a taxi so he stayed in his friend's house.

I knew his friend wasn't going to 'shop' on him. I didn't have proof, but I didn't believe the story one bit.

When you get them to tell the same story, it changes every time they tell it.

When I was younger and before mobile phones unfortunately, men could have got away with saying they had phoned you on your landline, but not now.

Towards the end of the relationship he began to go out more often with the lads than me. So that meant another night staying at his friend's house, apparently. One thing that always struck me was his friend was married, but I had heard rumours that he was having affairs. No smoke without fire. My late mother always said to me, 'show me your friends and I'll show you, you'. His friend wasn't up to much and I was beginning to see neither was he.

When I pulled him on a few lies he had told, he would just laugh. He thought it was hysterical that I had found him out. It just became one lie after another, until I could take no more, because I felt the whole relationship was a lie.

He always talked the good talk, but nothing ever seemed to materialise. He was apparently always applying for these highly paid jobs, but he never seemed to change jobs.

He always spoke in thousands when he was talking about money. But things didn't add up.

If he seems to be giving a lot of excuses, then you need to try and find out what is the truth and which isn't. When I have done a little digging in past relationships, I have always found the truth in the end. Time and truth will reveal all.

I remember an ex telling me that he was going on a lads' night out with his brother who was just home from America. Of course that was an excuse to get out on the 'pull'. When two different people were telling me they seen him kissing another girl, I thought there must be some substance to this. Plus, his history of being a ladies' man would back that up.

I knew a work colleague who never found out that her fiancé had cheated and ended up marrying him. Twenty years down the line, she eventually found out, because guess what, he continued to be a cheater even after he got married to this girl and had kids. Some of the women I know have decided to save their marriage and some haven't, but I often wondered if this girl ever knew how long her husband had been cheating on her or did she think it was a one off. He got away with it for so long because nobody could tell her what he was really up to, because they could see she was besotted with him.

My reason for not telling her was because I know nine times out ten the messenger always turns out to be the 'bad guy'. If my work colleague had directly asked me face-to-face, 'Have you heard my fiancé is cheating on me,' then I would ask her if she wants to hear the truth or does she want me to tell her what she really wants to hear? If she wants the truth, then I would categorically tell her all I know. Some people aren't ready for the truth. It's too painful to bear.

Would her life be totally different today, I would say absolutely, but it wasn't meant to be? Maybe somebody did come forward and tell her the truth, but I will never know. Plus, she has kids, so I'm sure she wouldn't change that for the world.

I know girls who have thought they were being the dutiful friend by telling their friend what everybody else knows about their boyfriend/ husband. In many cases, I have heard that the person that has been cheated on, cuts all ties with their friend and kept their boyfriend/husband. The messenger always gets shot.

The biggest 'porky' I was ever told was that my ex wasn't married when in fact he was. With the internet these days, you can find out so many lies. Especially on Facebook. Very little is private these days.

I know a girl whose new boyfriend's profile picture on Facebook was of him with his arm around a girl. When he was questioned, he said that's my sister. Of course he was found to be lying and had been seeing this other girl for two years.

Recently I was talking to a girl in her twenties, and she told me she had broken up with her boyfriend of two years. I said I was sorry to hear that, but she said it was best thing that ever happened. She found out he was lying to her. But sneakily enough, he had always seemed very upfront with his passwords, etc. until she noticed all messages and emails were deleted, so she knew he had something to hide.

I remember one of my ex's cousins came over from England, and they were reminiscing about their childhood. When one of the cousins said, 'oh do you remember you use to be such a liar when you were little?' I nearly choked. I began to wonder, was this part of his personality from an early age?

I know men who have spent their whole lives lying. It's a hard habit to break. Men who have had two lives which ended up in two families. Their wives never found out for years. One man is in his seventies, and his whole life was a lie. The strange thing was that he never left his wife of fifty years, but still supported his mistress and family. I wonder what gap is missing in their life, that they feel the need to lead two separate lives. He obviously felt he could do whatever he wanted regardless of his wife and children's feelings. Ironically, he would be a controlling husband, but it's a shame he didn't have some control in other areas.

So men that are guilty of lying can go on to be liars all through their lives.

'A man is known by the company he wants to keep'.

I think being a pathological liar has to be one of the worst traits someone can bring to a relationship. Integrity is so important because it covers so much of a relationship.

- Is he lying about his feelings for me?
- Is he cheating on me?
- Is he really working late or is he seeing someone?
- Is this relationship what I thought it was?
- Does he really want to commit to this relationship?

When you are dishonest in what you are telling your partner, then are you dishonest in other ways and you cannot be trusted full stop.

Maybe they are living in a fantasy world?

After a year, yes, I know I held on for a year when I should have left Mr Pinocchio earlier, the whole relationship just drained me and I became tired of trying to figure out whether what he was telling me was true or another lie.

After a person that has lied to you once, there is a pretty good chance they will do it again.

Some men that I have known, have made the most elaborate lies. The more elaborate the lie, the more they think they will be believed. If there's always some drama or excuse, then you know this is a pattern.

Are they stepping up to the mark in the relationship? If they are always making some excuse or story, why they haven't turned up or why they didn't phone, then he just wants to be somewhere else, or with someone else rather than you. Sometimes it's a hard tablet to swallow, but we have to get real. It is hurtful when we get rejected. Why be with someone who is always looking for an excuse not to turn up or be with you?

That doesn't mean there is something wrong with you. It's not your problem but his. He can't be honest and up front. It doesn't mean you won't find someone who wants to be with you, it just means he definitely isn't 'The One'.

He has done you a favour, because now you know what he's really all about.

Eventually there will be that person who won't lie to you, and does want to be with you and be part of your life. You want a relationship that has integrity and it's the relationship you know it is, not what you hope or think it is in your mind. Where there are no doubts in your mind, is he being true to me?

I know women who wouldn't take no for an answer, and practically stalked their boyfriends until they eventually married them. Who wants to be married to someone who liked them rather than loved them because they felt bullied or pushed into marriage?

Some men would say I love you, but I'm not in love with you. Like the song 'Two Out of Three Ain't Bad' by Meatloaf. Being with a dishonest person or a fake isn't very rewarding, it's a constant misery. It takes over your every thought and plays with your mind. They will only change when they want to change and not when you or anybody else says so.

I decided I couldn't cope any more. I couldn't prove he was being faithful; it was too much inner torment, having to question someone, day in and day out, to try and find out which part he was telling you was truth and which was lies.

I should have bought a lie detector and strapped it to him every evening, to find out what was true and what wasn't.

I would have saved myself a lot of hassle.

The lies that men tell women and what we want to hear:

- My second phone is for work.
- I have no idea who that girl is texting me.
- You're the love of my life and I would never cheat on you. (Their actions tell a different story).
- We need to slow down our relationship. It's going too fast (they want to break up).
- She's just a friend.
- Last drink for the road
- I'm not being distant.
- I'll call you
- I've never met anyone like you before
- That's not my hotel/jewellery receipt
- She is stalking me

- My wife and I are living under same roof but living separate lives.
- I'm staring at her because I recognise her from somewhere.
- I'm going on a lads' night out
- I have to work late a lot.
- I would never lie to you.
- You can trust me
- I left my phone in the car
- I only own one phone
- I had no signal on my phone
- I couldn't get a taxi
- I stayed at friend's house last night
- I am not the father of her baby
- I am not married
- She's my sister's friend
- A friend asked me to look on Tinder for him

Chapter 12
Mr Booty Call

What is a man saying when he phones you at one am, at the end of a night out? He has most likely been out at a bar and couldn't find a woman, so decides to phone you. If you are not good enough in his eyes to meet up in the day time, why would you jump to his tune in the middle of the night? 'But I'm using him too', I have heard girlfriends say.

Where's your self-respect? We all know men talk, and word gets around.

If you think he will change and eventually want to be with you, that's not going to happen. Any man will tell you there are the women that could be a wife and the women who will always be their 'Booty Call', if and when needed.

Block his number and move on to bigger and better things.

Don't get known as being 'easy'. But you can tell a lot by what way a woman dresses, what type of person she is. She's either classy or trashy.

I was at a wedding recently. A man who I know was also at the wedding, and he had brought his new girlfriend along. When she walked towards me as she was being introduced by a friend, I couldn't stop staring at her boobs. I saw her boobs before I could see her face. She didn't have massive boobs; it was the top she was wearing. It wasn't until afterwards, when I got talking to her, the personal questions that she was asking me about my past relationships left me very embarrassed, that I changed the subject and left the table. My first impression was right. Later my sister said to me that all our male friends and family, some of them single, some not, had commented on this girl, saying she's a bit of alright. They couldn't take their eyes off her. She wasn't overly attractive. Then my sister said men can smell a good-time girl a mile away. I was so shocked and realised how true that was. This girl had actually had an affair to be with this man she was at the wedding with. That says it all.

Nobody's perfect. But if you have humongous boobs, you don't need to highlight them by wearing a tight low top to show them off. If you're a woman, people will know that you are without having to draw attention to your feminine parts. They will speak for themselves covered up or not. Your personality should shine through, and let the first thing that people will see be your face and not your boobs.

By your outfit, you are going to draw a certain type of man to you.

Think Jackie Kennedy or Audrey Hepburn. In modern times, Kate Moss and Olivia Palermo. You can still be sexy and be covered up. Less is more.

As you get older, you realise mud sticks. When I was growing up, there were certain girls that did have a name for themselves. You will hear 'do you remember so and so, she liked the men'. When you're young, you don't think this is going to haunt you for the rest of your life.

I remember my mother and my auntie advising me on men. 'Don't give in to men because they only want one thing'. Thank goodness I was wise enough in that area. At the time I thought, what would they know? They are ancient and times have changed. I'm sure girls these days would think the same. But it's true for every generation. If you have no respect for yourself, you will end up with men who have no respect for you.

I remember one girl having sex outside a disco on the footpath. She was so drunk she didn't know what she was doing. I just felt pity for her. To this day people remember thirty years on what she did that night.

I don't care what anybody says, <u>MEN TALK</u>. They mightn't talk as much as us women, but they talk about 'types' of women they have been with.

That's what men do, they can't help themselves.

Women who take naked selfies, I have no doubt men will show their friends. It's all about the ego.

Recently I was going through Facebook and I came across a beautiful young girl, beautiful makeup, her hair was wet and she was lying in a bath. I was so shocked that this was sent out on FB for everyone to see. The message she was sending out to all the boys was 'look at me' and 'come and get me'.

Women forget that when they have children, they will regret these things later. Some things can never be discarded. They will stay with you forever.

Most of us like a small glass of wine, but when you have one too many and all your inhibitions go, well that can be dangerous. Especially when you can't remember a thing from the night before.

I have heard a lot women say, 'he has no respect for me'. If someone is going to speak unkind nasty words to you, then he doesn't care or love you the way he should.

I know we all want our relationships to work and we 'let a lot of things go' when it comes to addressing issues that are bugging us. Hurt can mount up and you will begin to resent your partner. But if you have never voiced your opinion and told him not to speak to you with that certain tone or use those words, and he continues, how is your relationship ever going to be pure and fulfilling?

We all need a 'soft' place to fall when we are going through tough times. That's what our partners should be, somewhere we can go and tell them how we are feeling. Especially if you lose a loved one, you need that support. A shoulder to cry on. A 'sounding board' to get rid of all your fears.

Your partner is either a 'drain' or a 'radiator'. If he feels like a noose around your neck and if you have discussed how you feel but are getting no support, tell him you aren't happy. Sometimes I have heard my husband say 'why didn't you tell me, I had no idea you were feeling like that'. You have to discuss it with your partner so there is a chance for things to change and improve.

It's half the battle in life if you have a good supportive partner.

An old friend of mine use to date all the 'wrong' types of men. We could see they were using her. On the outside, she was putting up a front and pretended she was happy. Her view was, any attention is better than no attention, even though men would hang around her, when they only wanted one thing.

I know a male friend of mine who met a really lovely girl. He was crazy about her. The one 'bug bear' he had, was that she slept with a lot of men. Because a lot of her exes lived locally and he knew who she'd been with, he couldn't accept or get it out of his head that she had been with them before him. Eventually they broke up. I can't say if that was the reason why, but it didn't work out anyway.

Start as you mean to go on. I know some men who have booty called women, then after a few months, the girl would fall for this fella. But eventually he would meet his 'future wife' and she was a long-distant memory. She was the one that ended up getting hurt. She went the wrong way about trying to get into a serious relationship with him. They had nowhere to go, because from the 'get go', he had sex on his mind, not about getting to know her or spending quality time with her. Whereas she really liked him. But if he wasn't into her from the beginning, the sex was only going to keep him for a while. In his mind, it was never going to be long term. There was no wooing in this relationship. Just sex.

We all make mistakes in life. Sometimes we learn from what experiences other women go through. Being on the outside looking in is so much clearer. When you know better, you do better.

Women give free sex because they are trying to keep him by her side. This is only temporary. If he was any way serious about you, he would be investing in this relationship. He would be taking you out and treating you like you were the most precious thing he had ever found.

A lot of women wear their heart on their sleeve, and our idea of where the relationship is going, could be a hundred miles away from what the man is thinking.

If he booty calls and you give in, then he will never take you seriously and you will never know how he really feels, because he hasn't earned you yet. It will never move on, from this just sex stage. That's as far as it will go.

While he's having sex with you, he is bidding his time until Mrs Right comes along.

Chapter 13
Mr Married Man

If a man ever marries his mistress, a vacancy is left. Mr Married Man likes to have his cake and eat it.

Some women see married men for the thrill. Sometimes it's the holidays or the gifts they receive.

She will never be truly happy.

Most mistresses hang on to the hope that one day he will finally leave his wife. Married men who cheat are deceitful. They promise their mistress what they want to hear. Most promise that they will eventually leave and they are just waiting for the 'right time'.

Why would a man buy a cow when he's getting his milk for free?

You will only ever be second best in his life. If he's unfaithful to his wife, he has the potential to be unfaithful to every woman he ever has a relationship with. It's in his DNA. He is a thrill seeker. They don't think about the consequences or the people they are going to hurt.

In some cases, the men are going through a mid-life crisis.

Very few married men leave their wives for their mistress and any that do, eventually return to the marital home.

It a pointless road. I have known a few women who have had affairs with married men and when the man leaves his wife, the mistress can never rest easy, for she will follow him, for fear the same will happen her.

Once a cheater always a cheater.

I knew a man who was a renowned cheat. His wife was the last to find out. Unfortunately, one of his sons turned out exactly like the father. He had numerous relationships but was never truly content and happy with one woman. His father died a lonely man.

Mr Married Man is good at keeping you hanging on. He calls the shots, whether you want to believe it or not.

He is the one pulling the strings and you are dancing to his tune. You will always be second best.

Very few men will leave their wives, especially when they have kids, because they know they will only have fifty percent custody.

Some women will say, you can't help who you fall in love with. But a married man will never be truly yours. Integrity is the foundation of a relationship. The only way is down, in a relationship born from deceit.

Your life will be an unpredictable waiting game and the married man is at the helm.

A friend told me recently about a girl she knew who had met a married man with a child. He had told her his marriage was over. She believed him. He told her everything she wanted to hear and she fell for it. He went to her father to ask for her hand in marriage. Her family thought he had done the decent thing by asking her father, but behind it all, they weren't convinced because he was known for having a bad reputation. Wedding plans had been made but no matter what her family done, they couldn't convince her to leave him. Word got around that he was still married.

Her family were devastated. Then she got pregnant. As soon she told him, she never saw him again. He had conned everybody and never had any intention of marrying her. You can imagine how distraught she was.

Thankfully her family rallied around her and helped her through having the baby.

The poor girl could never have foreseen what was going to happen, she was only in her twenties and believed everything he told her. How cruel.

Unfortunately, it's a chance you take when you meet someone, unless you know otherwise, of course you are going to believe what they tell you. In a relationship, you build trust and it's so disheartening when you find out the contrary.

As you get older, you are more tuned in and mostly you can tell when someone is leading you up the garden path.

Hindsight is a great thing.

As you get older, you don't take things at face value as much.

Some married men may tell you that he and his wife live under the same roof but have no relationship but this is most likely another lie.

When a married man is buying you holidays or diamonds, he is buying you. He may as well hand you a wad of notes.

If he were truly in love with you, he would have already left his wife. His intentions will never change. And why would they when he has two women in his life? He will be content with going along with the way things are for as long as he can.

You are delusional and hanging on to a dream that will turn into a nightmare eventually.

When you need this married man, he will never be able to support you emotionally in your life. It is a lonely relationship being with a married man, because they can never be in your life when you need them, because his wife or children will be his first priority no matter how you feel.

I used to work with a girl who was seeing a married man. Everybody knew she was seeing him yet she seemed to be oblivious to this. She would go on holidays, but we never saw any holiday photos. At times she seemed unhappy, and I'm sure she felt strange when we were talking about our relationships, but for a few years she led everyone to believe she was single. That was thirty years ago. She eventually married someone else. She will always be seen as the eighteen-year-old girl who had an affair with a married man.

It is a selfish thing because no one is thinking of his wife or kids. If the mistress put herself in the shoes of his wife, would it be so easy to have the affair?

Some men seek the thrill.

I remember before I met my husband, I was out at a disco and a mutual friend introduced me to this fella. I knew he was well known for cheating on his wife. We started chatting, and then he asked me for a slow dance. I nearly had a heart attack. I promptly said no. He asked me why. I said, 'Do I need to remind you that you are a married man and I think you should go home to your wife and kids and grow up'. He said, 'She's not at home, she's in Donegal. I left her and the children there today'. I couldn't believe my ears. He left them there and drove back down the road home again. I was so shocked. I said to him 'I've heard enough'. I thought that poor girl, not long after having a baby. I just felt for her.

He was so oblivious to what he was doing. Or else he knew and just didn't give a damn. It was hard to believe that someone could be so cold.

The shocking thing about this was this fella done this in a small town, where everybody knew him and her family. He just didn't seem to care. When he was telling me she was in Donegal, he was so 'matter of fact' about it all. No shame.

I thought to myself I must be leading a very sheltered life, is this what really goes on?

Some married men have no shame and have no cares about another person's feelings. They want a good time and don't care who gets hurt.

Another night I was out, and a group of fellas where out on stag night out. I knew one of the fellas and one of his friends tried to kiss me. Of course I moved away. He was full as a coot. I said, 'What do you think you are doing?'

He just wanted a kiss.

I said, 'Have you lost your memory? What's that on your left hand second finger?'

'That doesn't mean anything,' he said.

'Clearly not,' I said, and I walked away.

Drink in and wit out.

If a man is always on a 'lads' nights out', there is something amiss. Maybe he still wants the single life. You can't have two feet in different camps.

Some men never grow up.

Chapter 14
Mr Online Dating

I hadn't planned on writing a chapter on this subject until I turned the television on one day and heard a woman talking about her experience of online dating. The guy she met seemed to her, very easy to talk to and had a great sense of humour. He asked if he could meet up with her and they went for a meal in a lovely restaurant. She had a great evening with him and at the end of the night, he asked her to go back to his house to watch a movie. She declined and said that she didn't want to go. Her gut instinct was that she didn't feel comfortable with going back to his house, as she had just met him. She said he kept reassuring her it was just to watch a movie. He was quite pushy about it and she felt he kept insisting on her going. She finally gave in. When they got back to his house, he attacked and raped her.

I was so horrified for her. She knew her gut instinct was not to go. He kept trying to convince her that it was okay to go to his house, because 'it was just to watch a movie'.

This is a lesson for all of us. If someone won't accept 'no' for an answer in any situation, don't give in, because they are being pushy for a reason. We have to get assertive and be firm in our answer to get the message across. If they won't accept 'no' for an answer, then walk away.

This man was beyond manipulative but was very charming and convincing to this woman.

I remember being in a situation where 'no' was not being accepted for an answer. This man kept trying to persuade me into a situation I did not want to be in. After the third time of trying to get 'no' across to him, I raised my voice and said very firmly, "What part of the word 'no' do you not understand?" He stopped in his tracks and walked away. If a man sees you aren't going to take this manipulative abuse, he will soon back down. I know in cases of potential rape this most likely will not work. Some men mistake niceness for weakness. If someone is hounding you to change your mind, there is something unnerving about that. When someone won't accept your decision, it's manipulative and controlling.

I do not relish talking about rape, but people are more aware now and willing to talk about it.

Thirty years ago I remember two friends telling me they were raped by long-term boyfriends. At that time, I was naïve and so shocked. Oh my goodness, this can actually happen even when you're in a relationship. I know one thing, I never, ever forgot this. It just made me more aware and more careful in the situations I got myself into. But how do you protect yourself, when it's someone you think you know? I couldn't get my head around this. As I have got older, I'm aware it happens in marriages too. Someone who is supposed to be your friend and sole protector.

I was in a situation once, when I was in one of my controlling relationships. I was told by my partner he was going to rape me. He had got into a rage about something, and to teach me a lesson, this is what he was going to do. I cannot tell you the fear those words conjured up in me. I just remember thinking my life is over now. The only thing worse than rape to me is dying. He pulled me onto the bed. I always thought in a situation like that I will do this and that. Reality isn't as kind. At the last minute, he changed his mind. I was in such shock. I was one of the lucky ones, and I'm sure what happened to me very rarely happens. He must have come to his senses and his conscience got the better of him. One thing is for sure, I never forgot what happened, and I often think what could have been.

Rape does happen in marriage, and down through the centuries women had to obey their husbands in the bedroom. They didn't have a choice. Not so long ago, you were told, 'you've made your bed and you have to lie in it.'

It's shocking to think that women felt trapped in a marriage and some were treated like slaves. It was seen by men, that was their duty to please the man. Women had no voice.

Thankfully, it doesn't have to be that way anymore. Women have a choice now not to stay. There are so many organisations that help women leave these horrifying situations and build a new life for themselves. There is so much hope now. The most difficult part is making the decision to leave. Even though leaving is the most critical time for a woman.

Millions of women have come out the other side, picked themselves up and turned their lives around. They have got careers and built a new life for themselves.

I am one. I am proof. I was fortunate that I didn't have kids. But I know people who have left with their kids and they have never looked back. They may never forget what they experienced, but they are able to eventually move forward.

I don't want to scare monger, but in any situation in life, to be forewarned is to be forearmed.

Online dating has some positive outcomes. I know of two women who met their husbands online dating. They are now very happily married with kids.

It's about being aware and not getting yourself into a situation where you have no control.

Tell friends and family where you are going and who with.

Online dating can also be a hive for scammers.

Be careful;

- If he doesn't give you his full name and number after your first meeting. He has something to hide.
- They target older women for money.
- If they seem to be moving the relationships very quickly.
- If they talk about money a lot.
- He can change his profile to the same interests as you. You could think you have found a perfect match.
- Does he seem too good to be true early on?
- Does he try to get you back to his house or go to yours?
- Meet in a public place and get your own way home.

Chapter 15
Mr Micro Cheat

A micro-cheat is someone who is a sneaky, subtle, low-key cheater. They might not actually sleep with another woman, but it's like being emotionally involved with them and building up a relationship. They aren't being completely faithful as far as being exclusively committed to their partner. They can have female companions that are as close, as you are to him. Obviously they have no idea how close they really are.

This has been a hot topic recently for my girlfriends and I. Is a micro-cheat really a cheat or is it all harmless fun?

If your partner doesn't know about your texting etc. to someone else, then in my eyes that's a cheat. What's the next step?

My experience of a micro-cheat was when an ex was very protective over his mobile phone. He always took it with him everywhere. Even into the bathroom when he was having a shower. I always knew something was up. So one night he got extremely drunk and collapsed into bed. I immediately thought 'mobile'. I felt it was my right to check his phone, as he was supposed to be in a committed relationship with me. So if he wasn't up to something, then what did it matter. I waited until he was 'out for the count'. When I checked his messages, sure enough, he was flirting away with this girl. 'you looked hot today in work'. I couldn't believe what I was reading. I tried to convince myself it's just harmless fun. Then it went on to read, 'I can imagine you in hot sexy underwear.' Then everything changed.

Of course when I approached him about it, he attacked me verbally for 'checking up on him.'

My pet peeve is 'it's nothing, your making something out of nothing'. The fact that if they don't take time to sit down and speak to you about your worries, then does he really care much for you in the first place? Especially if you are saying 'look, this has really disconcerted me, can we talk about where our relationship is going, and do we have a future together?'

I just told him if you knew I had texted some guy the same thing, what would you say to that? He just told me he trusted me and wouldn't think anything more about it. I said, 'Yeah, I believe you.' Needless to say, I ended the relationship soon after that episode.

Well, I couldn't trust him anymore, and I would be tempted to check up on him, and what type of relationship is that?

I think a lot of women try to tell themselves, well, they haven't actually slept with anyone. In the media these days we hear of quite a few celebrities caught sexting. I think it's one step away from having that 'affair'.

I have been in bars where my exes have made me feel uncomfortable, by seriously flirting with other women, as if I'm invisible. It is so disrespectful and rude. It's the way they talk and look at these other women. It is so demoralising. Of course they will tell you, they were just talking and it doesn't mean anything.

Your relationship with him is the same as all the other girls he knows. There is nothing exclusive or unique about your relationship. He is a real ladies' man and he needs female company and reassurance constantly. One woman in his life is never fulfilling enough.

They still keep in contact with their exes, and that used to drive me mad. It just doesn't make sense. I always thought the whole point of being an ex-girlfriend was that you moved on with your life, with no further contact with them.

If they are hiding those types of things, and they seem to have no morals or integrity, then where does a relationship end up without that trust? Especially if you are firm in your beliefs and you want an honest person to spend the rest of your life with.

Signs of a Micro-Cheat

- You have caught him on Tinder
- He has lots of female friends
- He flirts with every woman he meets
- He confides in a female friend more than you
- He deletes messages from female friends when you know they have contacted him.
- He keeps his mobile with him everywhere
- You find he has a second mobile hidden.
- You haven't met his friends
- He talks about one girl constantly

Micro-cheats will tell you that you are over-reacting when you confront him about text messages. He will probably say it's a bit of harmless fun.

Chapter 16
Mr I'm Always Right

We all love to be right – right! The whole point of an argument is to convince the other person, and to get him/her to see your point of view, and that you are right and they are wrong.

How do you compete with a competitive Mr I'm Always Right? You don't!

I think it's impossible, for the simple reason somebody has to back down, or else it could escalate into something nasty.

When I was seeing a Mr I'm Always Right, we were about four months into our relationship. Everything seemed to be going well, until one night we were, as I thought, discussing something trivial. We hadn't even raised our voices. Looking back, I think it really got his back up, because I was so calm and it wasn't a big deal to me. He would not let up and insisted on trying to get me to change my opinion. I finally said it doesn't matter that you have one view and I have another, and he slapped my face. Talk about being stunned. I thought I was dreaming and I remember thinking this can't be happening. When this had never happened to me before, and it is the most debilitating thing I ever felt. It was like an out-of-body experience.

He burst into tears and was so devastated at what he had done. This was another shocker. I then had to calm him down, and he promised to never do this again. Of course years down the line and talking to other women, they would say the same thing happened to them. It's all text book. I have never heard of a man saying he will never hit, kick or punch someone again and keep that promise. It just doesn't happen. It seems to be the first stage of a gradual catalogue of violent episodes.

I was talking to a girl recently, and she confided in me, that her new boyfriend was very argumentative and no matter what her point of view was, he was always talking her down. She thought that was okay. She told me that he would get jealous of her son sometimes, because the two of them had such a close bond, and he would try to get her to have the boy stay at his grandmother's more. I felt sick for her, because I knew what was coming. She told me a few other things and alarm bells were ringing. I just had to speak my mind and warn her. I said, 'You know he sounds very argumentative and controlling and I used to have a boyfriend like that.' I told her, that to me, it's the beginning of a cycle. She asked me was I still with him. I said no. I told her eventually over time, when I wouldn't agree with something he said, he began to slap me, and then it escalated into serious violence. I told her this is not good, because being argumentative is just the beginning, the next stage is hitting or slapping. She went very quiet. I didn't know if he had already done that yet, but I just told her, please be very careful, for you and your son.

A year on I found out that her boyfriend had beat her up and police were called. I was so hurt for her, because violence takes your mind, your spirit and the essence of who you are as a person, and just throws it in the gutter. You are at your lowest low.

I'm glad this girl got the courage to leave him, because it's harder to leave than it is to stay. It takes every ounce of courage you have.

I knew a girl who was married for twenty-five years to her partner and he never once said sorry, even if the argument or situation was totally his fault. She decided just to put up with it for an 'easy, quiet life'. Fair enough, she had children and just came to the conclusion that this was his way, and she knew at this stage he was never going to change. No matter what the situation was, he turned it around and made it her fault. She would tell me, well, he's a good father, hard worker, but when it came to disagreements, he could only see one side and that was his own.

Some people are obsessed about being right. They have to get the last word.

Sometimes you have to ask yourself, do you want to be right or do you want to be happy?

I know a couple, and the man would argue a black crow was white. I remember talking to his wife one day, and I said to her, why is it important for some men to always be right? Her reply was 'he's nuts'.

I burst out laughing. 'Are you serious?' I said.

'It's the only explanation,' she said. 'He is two sandwiches short of a picnic.' She's probably right. You don't argue with crazy. His brain must be wired wrong. She told me most of the time, she lets him rant away, because she says she's fighting a losing battle. It's pointless fighting with someone who in their mind is always right.

They go on and on, until they convince you to see their point of view, it means that much to them.

I remember an argument with two people I know, where both insisted that they were right. There was a fall out for a few years. When one of them became very ill, even though their family tried to reconcile them, the well man was more interested in being right than making amends with his very ill friend.

On the day of that argument, emotions were heightened and sometimes people take it out on the ones they are closest to.

In some cases, it could be a personality clash.

I remember getting directions to a place I needed to go to from a married couple who I was friendly with. The two of them gave me different directions. She was telling me turn left at the crossroads and he said no, you turn right. It turned out they were giving me directions from different directions. They were both right, in that he was giving me directions from his house, and she was giving me directions from my house. That's says a lot about misunderstandings.

In a relationship, you have to pick your battles.

When I was in a relationship with a Mr Always Right, it nearly drove me crazy. After a while it wore me down. He would argue for hours, to convince me his argument was right. I thought to myself, you need to get a life. Obviously it was part of his 'thing'. He was always right. Everybody had to see his point of view because his was the right one.

In his mind, there was no room for another point of view.

Chapter 17
My Final Word

My Mr as near to perfect as I can get, may not be yours and vice versa. It's about finding someone who is compatible with you. I was once told that everybody's experience of the same person can be totally different, but you have to ask yourself, is this person making me happy with no, ifs or buts? It is like having four people around a table and observing an object in the middle. There are going to be four different opinions on what they see, and everyone's interpretation is going to be different.

I think I have kissed every shape and type of frog.

These are my views that went on in these relationships. It's just my opinion. What I felt I was going through. Some of my exes may think I'm Mrs Asperger's, Mrs Controlling or a Mrs Scrooge. We all have faults. A few of mine are I talk too much. I'm very untidy and can be highly strung. But they are cancelled out by my husband, who is the 'quiet man', untidy and very calm. Ha-ha!

So maybe this is the reason why our relationship works, because we cancel each other out.

Looking back, I have come to the conclusion I 'forced' fate into what I wanted, in my first marriage. That didn't happen. I didn't take time to get to know that person, and the facts of what being married to someone involved. I just wanted to get married. At the time I thought I was being real with myself. I wanted something that wasn't there in the first place and was never going to be.

All these men had good qualities as well. That's why it's so confusing at the time. Ultimately their bad qualities outweighed the good. The sad times outweighed the happy ones.

If you get that sinking feeling sometimes, when your partner speaks to you in a certain manner or tone, and that doesn't make you feel good, then you need to ask yourself some serious questions.

Of course no relationship is perfect. It's about asking yourself is this fixable, or are you fighting a losing battle?

I have seen in a lot of cases where sons repeat the same pattern that their fathers have done. E.g. womanising and verbal and physical abuse.

It can happen to the best-reared child. Teaching them young, to talk about their feelings and controlling their temper is part of it, such as saying 'words aren't for hurting and hands aren't for hitting'.

They choose to be that type of person when they are an adult or they can do something about it. This can be achieved by taking stock and knowing they are doing wrong. Men who are abusers are getting something out of it (as Dr Phil would say, 'what's your payoff') otherwise they wouldn't persist in doing the same thing over and over again. They get into a rage that they can't control.

If your partner crosses the line and doesn't make you feel 'your better self', it will deplete you over a period of time, 'til you are a shell of your former self, and your spirit is demised.

Nobody's perfect, but hopefully with age comes wisdom, and with wisdom less drama.

Finally, when I asked ten of my friends and acquaintances, who have either had broken marriages or broken relationships, looking back, they all said that all the signs were there in the early stages of the relationship, and that they should not have continued with the relationship. For whatever reason, they took the risk and continued to stay in their relationship for a while, until the signs became reality.

One positive thing I can take from all the negative relationships I've had, is that when I went into the next relationship, I was more aware of some things that I didn't want in this new relationship and knew exactly what I did want. I stayed away from the same type of relationship I had before.

We can learn from each relationship so that we don't repeat history again.

You pick yourself up, like millions of women have done before you, and never give up. If I had given up, I never would have found my true happiness, nor have my two beautiful and challenging boys I have today.

Sometimes I get 'off days,' and I feel I can't see the woods for the trees, but I know God has a plan for all of us. It may not be exactly what we had planned in our minds.

When I was in these past relationships, I always tried to remember, that the darkest part of the night is just before the dawn.

Be patient to meet your Mr Right, and it will be the greatest investment you ever made. Illuminate the frogs, and in time, your prince will be revealed.

Frogs are the stepping stones to your prince, but a true prince will treat you like a princess.

When I think back to the Oscar Pistorius trial, it brought back a lot of bad memories for me. In my past toxic relationships, I would run to the bathroom and lock myself in. It was a place of refuge for me. I always thought that I could stay in the bathroom for a while, until things cool down and then I could leave.

When I said I was leaving the relationship, because it was too volatile, I would start packing to leave and all hell would break loose. I learnt early on, you never tell a volatile man you are leaving the relationship. It is the most crucial part of a violent relationship. They see 'red' when you mention leaving. 'If they can't have you, then no-one can.' That's their take on it. You are like an object to them, not a human being, and you belong to them.

I left a violent relationship a couple of times. When I returned, the violence was worse than before because he was so angry that I left in the first place. When I finally left for good, I would forget how bad it was when I was away from him, all the good times would come into my head. So when I thought of going back, I would visualise in my mind actually going in through the front door again, and reality would hit me, and thankfully I never returned. This worked for me.

When I met my second husband, it was worth the wait, and my patience paid off. We were together for four years before we got married. I didn't rush fate, the relationship was natural and just flowed. We certainly had our mountains to climb, but we worked out a path – together and conquered it. As long as both parties put in 100%, and are willing to work at the relationship.

Like every relationship, we are a 'work in progress'.

Life isn't perfect, and neither is any relationship. Everyone has a story to tell.

Nobody is trouble free this side of the grave. It's how you deal with each problem, head on, together. If you decide to stay single, there is nothing wrong with that either.

'Guard your heart above all else, for it determines the course of your life.'

A quote from *Proverbs 4:23*

And Finally

What you can tell from your first date.

Run a mile if:

1. He constantly talks about his mother
2. He gets extremely drunk
3. He gets bit agitated if you disagree with his opinions
4. He makes you pay
5. He orders the wine and chooses your food for you
6. He comes across as arrogant and self-righteous
7. He lets you find your own way home
8. He tells you he would love to have kids and you don't, vice versa
9. He gets jealous if you talk to the waiter for too long
10. He scans the room and gets distracted by other women in the room
11. He interrupts you and doesn't ask anything about yourself
12. He complains about the prices in the bar/ restaurant
13. He's dressed like he was going to work in the fields

14. He hasn't had a recent haircut.
15. He doesn't smell nice
16. He hasn't shaved
17. He makes very little eye contact
18. He keeps talking about an ex-girlfriend
19. He keeps sneakily looking at your covered up breasts
20. He turns up late
21. He talks constantly about his cat/dog
22. He is over confidant/arrogant
23. He talks about money and boasts about how he made his first million
24. He gets into a fight
25. He forgets his wallet
26. He talks about his time in prison
27. He constantly on the phone/texting
28. He dirty talks
29. He talks about himself excessively
30. He shovels his food into like there's no tomorrow
31. He tells you he prefers threesomes
32. He talks about his OCD
33. He talks about his constipation and bowel problems
34. He tells you about his three ex-wives.
35. He tells you he gets very annoyed at women who don't give him a second date
36. He tells you his ex-girlfriend/wife got a restraining order out on him
37. He tells you how much has won on gambling
38. He goes to AA
39. He's been to anger management
40. He hates his mother

41. He thinks married women should stay in the home and do all the cooking/cleaning etc.
42. He doesn't hold the door open for you or let you through the door first
43. He thinks he's God's gift to women
44. He is constantly visiting the bathroom
45. He believes in open relationships
46. He finds it difficult to stay monogamous
47. He doesn't seem to have basic manners and respect for women